I0617175

THIRD MAN BOOKS

Rachelle Toarmino

Published by
Third Man Books, LLC
623 7th Ave S
Nashville, Tennessee 37203

Art direction: Jordan Williams, Amin Qutteineh
Cover/book design: Amin Qutteineh

REGULAR EDITION

ISBN: 979-89-89908-97-4

THIRD MAN BOOKS

thirdmanbooks.com

Contents

MUSIC

Hell and Back 3

Real Romantic 4

Normal Neurotic 6

Sucker 7

Traitor 8

Top Answers.. 9

Utter 12

Midnight Animal 13

Disclosure from Mars.. 14

Heartbeast... 15

Fool Enough... 16

Con Te Partirò 18

Good Thing... 19

Birthday Forever 20

All My Life, Oh Lord... 21

Selected Poem of Frank O'Hara 23

You Like That 25

Flowers, Poems, Flower Poems................................... 26

FLOWERS

Common Senses 31

Killer.. 34

Center of Attention... 37

Pilgrim Soul... 40

Not Feeling It 43

Freak Accident... 46

Touch Identify 49

I Have My Limits 52

Lyric Lesson... 55

Grave Ratio 58

MEAT

Announcement... 65

Comeback 66

Rachelle Toarmino 76

for anyone

If we're all wrong about everything, the life so short and the craft so long to learn, the assay so hard, so sharp the conquering, the dreadful joy that passes so quick and then being left alone again, what I mean is love astonishes my feeling with its wonderful working so ardently so painfully that when I'm thinking about such certainty I don't know like the earth if I'm floating or sinking.

–Bernadette Mayer

I dont wonder that the good angels weep—and bad ones sing songs.

–Emily Dickinson

MUSIC

FLOWERS

MEAT

Hell and Back

Maybe I'm not a party
I approximate myself on all fours
I am like this   reacting like this

This is my body   take it
Having made it so real
I broke it for you

I income thusly into contact
     with beautiful reasons

Come any closer
I can't keep myself to myself

This music is touching
and mine is a tongue

and a tongue around nothing
     rings

Real Romantic

You feel like such a bonus
meeting me where I'm at

Nothing pleases me like life
in quotes in an obit

The impulse toward the lyric
is a private thing
and I'm a real insider

The sentence pulled back by its hair
settles into a miraculous
decoy for sense

Try telling a romantic
it's not as real as it feels

I get hopeful
looking the part

So what if love is my form

Love is first of all
and the rest of it all also

I unnerve for you

wanting to go all the way
but I haven't

Quick question
What do you want from me

Short answer
You can have it

Normal Neurotic

I get up it's another day. Put on
            the good bra
for no one. Tight corners.

Curled and oiled. Dressed
            to drown
into my own mouth. It's another day

dreaming into myself. I think
            I dream myself.
Having wasted nothing of what I feel

I blank like film in light. It is hard
            for me to give up
the world. I am hard on me. I give up

the world. My science stilled
            in parentheses
in all these unplayed lines.

Wanting not what's music enough
            but some way
to say whatever and specific.

Flora, fauna, weather. Fat
            on the tongue
salt in the brain. And my freakish

heart whether you want it
            or not. And my
freakish heart if you want it.

Sucker

Can't tell unless I squint
whether his shirt says money
or honey. Sweet hell.
So he wants his email to find me
well. I spend most days mad
and I've learned to like it.
Red everything.
It's nothing short of a pleasure
for you to find me. Well
there I go again taking
what I can get and giving
it all I've got. What I've got
is my voice and heat breaking
against it. It's nothing
to know how hot a voice can be.
I'm told the opposite
of money is waiting
of honey is no honey. Unless
I've got anywhere better to be
I'll play together nicely. Even I
want me to have a great weekend.
Would you look at that.

Traitor

Now what   now that
it's not what   it looks like

For you I keep   my fingers crossed
and cleaned   behind my back

I pull back   the paywall
looking   for answers

I am an American

Again I guess   the meaning right
of traitor   on my quiz

Is it personal

You put your money   where my mouth is
making it   personal

Now that I'm not   what I look like
winning you   back

For you I leave   on all the lights
They play   my favorite trick

My eyes unbelieving it   blink

Top Answers

Cry of a cat?
meow

Cry of a horse?
neigh

Cry of surprise?
aha

Cry of a dog?
I don't know if it counts.

Do anteaters cry?
no they do not CRY!

Do pelicans cry?
technically pelicans do cry but they cry through their noses!!

Do men cry?
I have seen men cry.

Cry of the unborn child?
What would you like to know about it?

What do you do when a dog loses its bark?
you cry and cry and cry then take it outside

How do you make a dog bark?
you push the bark button push the bark button

How can you tell if someone is going to cry?
their eyes are swelling and their throat sounds off

How can I lose my voice without crying?
Get a friend to punch you in the throat.

How do I make my cry better and louder?
scream from your stomach and let your inner scream out

What is a scream?
It is a thing. AND an action.

What is another word for scream?
maybe you should just describe it?

Is a scream a ghost?
no. a scream is a scream even if it is screamed in a "haunted" place.

What happens if you scream near a ghost?
you are doomed

What names shouldn't you call a ghost?
I do think it's a tad disrespectful to arbitrarily name a ghost.

Do animals name each other?
plenty of animals can speak FOR THEM SELVES!!!

Can animals communicate with each other?
yes! animals communicate with each other in their own animal talk

Why do animals communicate with each other?
for safety and reproductive purposes

Why do animals echo?
because they need to be heard!!

Which animal voice has no echo?
the answer for this question is DUCK

Which animal voice has no echo?
the answer is....... well nobody really knows... the duck, by the way, has an echo

What is the future tense of echo?
I will echo. Hope this helps!

Utter

I go along with all of it.
Anyone can love

that I get to the good parts
keeping questions to myself

when we're by any means.
What good does it do to say it?

I am long for you, all the way
italic, but you're too war

when the situation is sur-
render and sweetly.

Call it total what goes on.
Call it an evening, even close.

Or if it's day that breaks
what is it light wants

the night to do.
I'm saying I want to happen

lifting as I warm.
But if it makes you happy.

Midnight Animal

All night like a man
that song wanted
my attention

A lie looks different
with the light on
and for what

What can be done with hurt
when I hum it into arrows
between two dreams
and breathless like an ellipsis

It takes a certain animal

I'm not   in on the joke
though you'd hardly know it
from looking at me

I know it like a feeling
I can be a little mean

Today was how many times
since that hurt got hot
beneath my tongue

It's how I sing so much

Disclosure from Mars

Don't say last nerve.
Don't say red

isn't my color. Rust, butterscotch.
I'll melt when it matters. Meaning yes

the way these syllables move
I won't shut up about. Watch me

husband around you. All of it
runaway and random. Okay but

I don't care when you take
my ideas. You're getting

my old ideas. I'm nobody's first love
but anybody's last. I come on too strong.

The long years of burning up
with wanting to say only it. Hey.

Heartbeast

The host on stage invites us to give it up
    one more time
as if to say surrender would will
the obvious   all that we have to give

We come to life uselessly
all the usual transaction fireworked
    into a patent finish

Maybe I have a thing about it
native to brass and warning
    and I   licked finger
warming the edge of a glass

It is a sound of neighboring
    this grand gut answer

    in which your fricative
and my fricative uprise
    into absolute   value

into same   music

We are so universal   yes
We echo   hear how far

We want to know what it's like
We want to know how it feels

We want to know what it's like
We want to know how it feels

Fool Enough

I feel personal
doing my own thing

I forget the details
handling them

Can't help I'm led by the ear
pinched by it

I take my attention
to distraction
as a kind of willpower

I want to be at least as ongoing
as a steak on a string

new as anyway
and no better for it

Inside's the longest way to look

not at the Moon but at Buzz Aldrin
whose mother's maiden name was Moon

Whose idea was it?

It strikes me simply
and thusly
each day how it is

The excerpts
the signal
the whole of it

How where there's light
there's heat
and where there's heat

you'll know it when you feel it

I'm trying to tell you
the rest of it

Con Te Partirò

When I am ill
I live on the horizon
I miss the light when there's no light
Words go missing from the room
When you are ill

Out the window
I tell everyone of my outgrown heart
Open your life wide and shut me inside it
This evening you've found
This odd little way

With you I leave this place
I've never seen or lived it anyway
With you I leave it
I live it with you
Not even noon can catch us
I live it with you

I say it over
I tell you of the want

I leave with you
I with you

Good Thing

We're a crowd again
for the love of it
no use for measure
making out your breath
in the midnight here
so sweet like flint
I cash in like whatever
heart the poem's for
I hope it does go on
or the honeyed throat
what goes with it knows
this is the tradition
I don't wonder what
makes a good thing
can't get over you
since you said time
means so much to me
all bright and first-person
the effect being to slip
into something less
particular sound of
whelmed for once
but I get out of hand
getting myself
out of your hands

What would I say of you
if I had to
say it all again

Birthday Forever

I love you shining in the sheets of our Saturday morning hangover. I call it flint about your wrist because it's one of my words for you. I think something about history but I'm alive and changing the subject, saying thanks like it's my birthday forever. Not that I believe everything should last forever but it's been interesting. I've got to live somehow, wanting you this one of many more weekends. I can't believe the first thing I said to you wasn't oh.

All My Life, Oh Lord

My father wants to know if we're "pay pals."

My father calls me on his birthday and says, "It's my birthday."

My father keeps a shoebox of greeting cards in his closet, pre-signed and "ready for anything."

My father tells my fiancé he'll stop sending me Valentine's Day cards if it, you know, means anything to him.

A woman's father might be the first man she loves.

My father invites one hundred and seven people to my wedding.

"I don't want to hear about that roleplaying shit," my father says to me when I try to talk to him about gender roles.

The brown lasiked eyes of my father fill with awe as "everything" on Pine Avenue changes in his lifetime.

On my father's nightstand: two books on horse racing, patchouli candle, note with *LUNCH WITH FRANKIE / CHAIN TO FIRTH'S / ITUNE?*

One night in the 1980s, one mile from the pharmaceutical plant and three from the one-hundred-and-sixty-seven-foot waterfall, my father accidentally becomes a father, my mother tells me.

My father's idol is not his father but the television actor his sisters tell him he looks like.

My father works with men who report him to management when he calls them "Benny!" and not Dr. Price.

My father wanted to work at the hospital and not the plant because he prefers people to machines. "Now everything's a machine," he tells me.

My father treats Siri like a Magic 8-Ball.

My father takes his iPad to Best Buy when he forgets his Facebook password.

My father creates an Amazon wishlist and adds "ideas" like *PEACE for all my FAMILY and FRIENDS* and *for my numbers to come in*.

My father speaks to his brothers in a voice I don't always recognize.

I speak to my father in a voice I receive but don't always understand.

My father when the server comes to take our order: "Get whatever you want."

Since 2008 my father's ringtone has been the hit single "In the Air Tonight" by Phil Collins. He answers singing.

Selected Poem of Frank O'Hara

Now that I am off my couch
I have no kindness left.
I am not interested in good.
                    I do what I want.
I am what people make of me.
      Hey, you! Is this love?
Whose heart is beating in this shell?
                They say I mope too much
        but really I'm loudly dancing,
surprising you with a party
from which I was the decoy.

You should go to bed with everyone
who looks at you. All life's fun,
desire's an exaggeration. No gods,
low thoughts, and an evil almost rockets.
            My heart is in my pocket.
    Oh my dear oh
                        how it is to be alive.

            I can't tell that I'm alive
        except I name the world.
I am never quiet. I mean silent.
Soon it is a whole page of words.
It's not for me, I'm not dead.
            I am alive with you.
        I would rather die
                for love, but I haven't.

If you were with me, if speech
were too awesome a gift and beauty
a thing you keep
                  moving. Stars are out.
Decide what you want of my name
and take it. Bear me toward a future
   which is not so—
                        Imagine!
I'll call you. Yes call me.
Love, Rachelle.

You Like That

Me being no one
it's everything to know you.

You'd like it if I said that.
You'd think it were so great.

Me being no one
I think you're such a dream

saying I'll take one of everything
calling me in from my own name.

All my favorite pop stars are singing
I want. Want you back

want your feeling I want
some more. I don't want to climb

into my only pair of high heels
looking like I own the place

but it's a start.
Not only love makes me bark.

Flowers, Poems, Flower Poems

A woman I've never met sends me tulips from two states over.
        There are things women know to do.

They sit on my desk next to the window. I love flowers
        because they're ordinary on one side of the glass

and a gift on the other. I keep them alive to remember I can.
        There are things women know how to do.

Clipped and caged and I think that's beautiful.
        What could be more feminine

than dying a slow death and another creature calling it
        beautiful. A hymn for every howl. It's crazy

when you think about it. Whatever you call it
        it's the one thing that brings me back into myself,

dancing naked in the mirror and making faces in the glass.
        I only ever wanted to make you feel my feeling.

You want to make me mad so you can call me mad
        well I am mad. You knew who I was

when you spun me like a prom queen and I kept my eyes
        open. I showed you my rotten nature.

A woman can spend her whole life spinning, arranging flowers
        and I intend to. Not now but I've decided to die

like a tulip in March on the desk of a stranger and opening.
        Sweet enough for you now? Still opening.

MUSIC

FLOWERS

MEAT

Common Senses

active dying is trending

the order of operations:
hunger is the first to go
listening   the last

three days later for the final cells

but we round down
following the heart's lead

/

/

I'll let you go
and I won't keep you—

two ways the father hangs up
the phone

nothing but powerlines
above open fields

of scrap metal and smoke

/

/

copper belongs to beauty

the way it sets an international standard
to which all other conductors
are compared

not nothing   beauty belongs
making us   in common

or if we use the telephone
life on either side

as good as any poem

long as the static
classic night

Killer

I never had a sexual
awakening

only an emotional one

the mother to the child
at the estate sale:

then don't touch
anything

you're afraid of!

/

/

each poem says   follow
my finger

then   made you
blink!

/

/

if it's true that
the flute and knife

are distant cousins

if each poem is
my fingers

in your mouth

Center of Attention

nothing turns me on like a lover
shouting my name in bed

to be onomatopoeically fuckable
and multiplied by one

that I mean
and therefore become

the average of   all data
instant of   very thing I am

/

/

the animation turns the system
into a spectacular disco

milky light versing
in and out of the blue

then again   fasting forward
makes any center of gravity

look like a target

/

/

I miss you is so accurate

the way I shoot out   all my feeling
toward a mark   I can't make

you know how it goes

to cross your arms
into a premature conclusion

Pilgrim Soul

in the beginning it was so good
to be still beginning

all of it plot-swept
and even
and exactly my near future

then a wild precedent dawned
making everything odd

/

/

a matter of time   and with that
he sank all odds for her to happen

the heart thickening   inside a plot
the size of a sweet pea   beside the point

/

/

still some ideas stick
inside a good question

bribed with interest: get rich quick!
become more   interesting?

my point being: I'm getting to it

going on
and on

Not Feeling It

air hunger: when the mouth gasps
in its last-minute want

to work   as usual

shout inside the dream: I go out
on my split   ends

for you!

/

/

now it's zero that's unrealistic

much more sensible to be a remainder
and close enough

this world and its heatwork
made by trying to break even

working with it
I say my goodbye on speaker

/

/

if we can't get this light on

if we can't make it right

can't see to the end
of this love

something borrows me
fully persuaded

Freak Accident

I luck into my material
like a room where people hide
waiting to shout
                    surprise!

today's signs: PLEASE COME IN
I'M OPEN

IN CASE OF CRISIS
SHATTER

/

/

I have my doubts finally

not to tell a strange world
flashlight under the chin

but to react   right-sized
and given   something to do

since I smell smoke
I buy flowers

/

/

since we're pointing fingers

it took an emergency for doors
to open   out
from the   inside

invent your life-giving vest
with your breath

PUSH

Touch Identify

suppose I sound like a factory
the way you make me repeat myself

then the idea is a follow-up feeling:

to want to go without saying
to say the least

/

/

when she hears her own sound
wave from the video

the cat sits up
splitting the difference

/

/

in fact I'll miss when a word
could open something

my impression: complete originality
yet no time to go into detail

let's say of vocabulary
we play ours out

let's say hell with it
treasure
good thing

I Have My Limits

if creating a constraint
is not unlike inventing problems

and I like to know my way around

then the limit toward which
all my desires reach

is pleasure   of impact

to feel the fact of my own voice
back itself against a wall

matter made by feeling
around in the dark

/

/

the mother gives the child
a box of crayons

meaning to keep her busy

she lines each along
the perimeter of the room

making a threshold of color

/

/

you want proof people love you
he says   telling me my problem

to go out on that kind of limb
index finger   holding blinds back

love gets me out of the house
love always gets me

out of the house

I am that woman
mouth open   ended

breath away

Lyric Lesson

I could handle the bonds
between feeling and hearing

but now it's the bicentennial
of feeling like and wanting to

touching is antique by comparison

many examples list music
though that's its second nature

/

/

listen: our appetites growl mouthward
addressing each other in subjunctive

/

/

all night crickets sound
the way glitter looks

light catching so rightly
we forget it's physical

all this to reach you

all this to say   what
eats me

Grave Ratio

again I get this feeling
to get even with life

lifting instants of world
into good view

felt   the material
gets its matte finish tenderly

by beating

/

/

if the force on an object
is equal to the weight of the material
moved by the object

it fails to make an impression

and floats

/

/

what I discover about gravity
is it figures my meaning

with its whole wanting
us to belong by each other

I press my life   against your life
can't keep myself   to myself

the heart   so gracefully clarified
lights on me—   it's meat

I open it
I use my teeth

MUSIC
FLOWERS
MEAT

Announcement

So thrilled to officially share that I have finally,
and among so many favorites, and my head is spinning.
Thank you! I am so pleased and psyched and geeked
and grateful. Friends, some personal news.
Please, a moment of your time. Happy! Join me!
Really hope you enjoy. The results are in
and I can't believe. So me of me to. I would.
I don't mean to brag but. An honor. I'm honored!

I have been hard at work to make you feel a way.
To make me feel a way. I do not want to die.
I want to wake each moment to the plain possible light
of language. I said I shared my flower poem
but it did not make me want to live. Thanks so much
for making this happen. And in such great company.

Comeback

What's so special about amusement parks is sometimes somebody dies on a ride you've gone on and suddenly you're a survivor because you didn't. It makes sense to hear the news and make it all about yourself: I can't believe it, I was just there, I know the exact turn they're talking about. Some rides get famous when guests come from all over to see the danger for themselves. I've been ready to risk it all for the world's steepest drop, for the bragging rights of having made it to the exit. What kind of question is truth or dare? The trick is you can always dare someone to tell a whole truth but me knowing nothing I always pick dare.

•

You can tell some women are survivors because they're around to say so, and you know what good for them. After the first summer of the virus a florist sang praise: Congratulations on surviving! Enter promo code SURVIVOR to enjoy 10% off your order. She meant grief is about the living but what if you're both, shouting from the exit: Come down from there! Look, I would if I could. I don't mean to be asking for anyone's attention. Not naturally a maximalist, never been one to suffer anything longer than I needed to. Still, I can't deny it's a beautiful view. No hands.

•

After the stabbing the husband swore confusion: But all I did was give her a few small nips! With nowhere else to go he was spotted by the neighbor, knife still hot in his hand. The artist took his testimony for the title of a painting. It helped her survive a crisis. With nowhere else to go a painting is an idea loosened from the body and left out to dry. I don't know how to talk about art, but there are things that I look at and I want to keep looking. With my back against the wall I said: First one to blink. Spoiled his trick, so what. It's interesting because I'm around to say so. Follow my finger. I want to show you something.

•

Red: Somehow the color for missing women. All the campaigns agree. They show me the color of don't and heat. Wrong but known, caught, corrected. Look what happens. Red makes a dare into attention, attention into data. It wasn't all that bad. When his hands shook in front of me I knew it was only practice. Heat holding back, a question asking when. Should we do it again? For some girls the worst ride is when you face each other and spin, but not for me. I come from a gaudy and gambling people. We like to watch. I like to see everything, even when I have to squint.

•

Who's laughing now? an acquaintance asks my post.
Just like that, the testimony is red. Nothing personal, no
longer mine. I'm told a body is no good at finding the
locations of injuries if they're inside it. No nerve to turn
the light on. That's why when some people have heart
attacks they feel something wrong not in their chest but
in their neck or jaw. Still, I have some questions. The
actress clutches her chest: I'm dying, she says. I'm dying,
they laugh. How she hates to be a joke she won't get
until later. But me I like to make you laugh. I like to
make you laugh so I can count your teeth.

•

It's not true what they say about thinking it'll never happen to you. In fact I made it look easy, you'd think I'd done it before. I didn't want to make it weird. It was nothing, nothing personal, and I thought nothing of it. What was it like? Like a fact, I don't remember. One in four chance. Where's the turn in that. What's true is you'll think you deserved it, but not because you asked. You think you're so special. You'd always wondered if you might be the kind of woman that wants bad things.

•

Tomorrow I'll be all imagination, no memory. Each new way of putting it feels like the first time I've put it. I tell myself I'm getting closer, each time I go around, still following every feeling out from a red wrong nothing. Living now is lasting, repeating. Everything multiplied and divided. Splitting makes one thing into many things. Meanwhile you're sick of hearing about it. I want to live because I want whatever's at the other end of that thought. It's a familiar tune, one that loops, losing breath like a gasp followed by another gasp. If the poem's the shape of a music box I'll spin it like one too.

•

I tried the whisper network and it failed me,
tried the public callout and it failed me,
tried playing nice, tried playing along,
tried graceful, tried grateful,
tried please, tried pretty please,
tried something you could do actually,
tried so appreciate you,
tried know I can trust you,
tried let me know what you think   I'm open,
                                        I'm flexible, I'm chill,
I'm cool, we're cool, I'm just happy to be here,
I'm around this weekend if you want to talk, no
worries if not, no pressure, no problem, no yeah
totally, don't sweat it, I get it, really I do, loud so loud
and clear.

•

I like the idea of playing it cool as much as the next girl but I just can't shut the fuck up. You miss me because I won't miss me and isn't that something. I've never understood that one comeback: Keep my name out of your mouth. It is in my best interest to take credit, to extend every feeling until it fevers into anything else. Having no idea left to loosen I intend to become the way you kneel. Like the poem I'll make you into something I leave behind so you do all the talking. No: Keep my name in your mouth. I'm tired but not sated. It is in my best interest to want to hear you sing.

•

I'm alive because I want whatever's at the other end of this song. She took it out of context, he said, and then they repeated. She took us out of context, they said, and then they repeated. Splitting makes one thing into many things. The artist took his testimony for the title of her painting. Look where that got her. All of us looking at it and her. I hear myself get closer each time I go around. Little songs the breath of whispers and losing like them too. Still, I have some questions asking when. We should do this again. I want— think you know it, don't you? Think you're so special you can tell what it is: I want. I want and what it makes me. That it does make me.

Rachelle Toarmino

I know a good thing.
When I love
I love hard.
I get weird for people
who don't want me.
No: I love
when I love hard.
I was born at night.
When red filled up
the air with light
I bet it felt like heaven.

Acknowledgments

Hell yeah to the editors of the following journals, who originally saw something in this work: *American Poetry Review*, *Bennington Review*, *Big Lucks*, *Iterant*, *Little Mirror*, *Poets.org*, *Salt Hill Journal*, *Shabby Doll House*, *Sixth Finch*, *Southeast Review*, *Spirit Duplicator*, and *Stone Canoe*. Hell yeah to Rusty Morrison and Omnidawn for publishing "Hell and Back" as a broadside and to Jake Rose for designing it; to Aidan Ryan and Foundlings Press for publishing "Comeback" as a booklet in *Strays Pack 4*; and to Rob MacDonald and Sixth Finch Books for publishing the poems in "FLOWERS" as the chapbook, *My Science*. And loudest, brassiest hell yeah to the team at Third Man Books—especially Chet Weise, Amin Qutteineh, and Justin Hargett—for their faith, fun, and small press excellence. Thank you all, from the bottom of my freakish heart, for doing what you do.

Hell yeah to Peter Gizzi, Hoa Nguyen, CAConrad, and Nick Sturm for taking the top of my head off with their poems—first of all—and for holding the door wide-open for mine with their generous advance praise. Hell yeah to the many other poets, artists, and familiars whose language incites mine, especially Sommer Browning for her poem "Great Things from the Department of Transportation," after which I wrote "All My Life, Oh Lord"; Molly Brodak for her poem "Molly Brodak," after which I wrote "Rachelle Toarmino"; and Julianne Neely for her chapbook-length poem *afFect theory*, from which I borrow her line "I said I wrote the flower poem but it did not make me want to live" and riff on it in "Announcement." It is a gift to correspond with you all.

Hell yeah to the MFA for Poets & Writers at the University of Massachusetts–Amherst for the opportunity to learn and write this book. Hell yeah to my teachers for pushing and putting up with me, especially Peter Gizzi, my game-changer; Hoa Nguyen, my gobsmacker; and CAConrad, my hero. Hell yeah to my classmates and friends in awful, interesting, and beautiful New England for making me and my poems better, especially Lucy Xiang-fu Wainger, Jayson Keery, Caroline Rayner, Colin Drohan, Nellie Prior, London Beck, Scout Turkel, Riley Jones, Tom Carlson, Sammy Lê, Cleo Abramian, Layne Eckensberger, Meagan Masterman, Elle Longpre, Mathias Svalina, and many others. Hell yeah to the Codependent Study independent study for keeping me honest and to Pure Barre Northampton for keeping me humble, or vice versa. Hell yeah to Ellen for the flowers. Special hell yeah to Francis Lo.

Hell yeah to everyone else who got weird with me during the making of this book: my home bases Julia Mariacher, Julianne Neely, Shelagh Dolan, Sarah Sgro, Rose Wells, Spencer Williams, Janet McNally, Joel Brenden, Noah Falck, Joshua Thermidor, Levi Van Cleve, Ana Vafai, and Robert D. Pohl; my *Peach Mag* co-conspirators Jakob Maier, Liz Bowen, Aeon Ginsberg, Kelly Xio, Sennah Yee, Yaz Lancaster, Rax King, Sebastian Castillo, Richard Chiem, RE Katz, Chux Camuglia, Mickey Harmon (forever), Shayna Kiblin, Bre Foster, and Matthew Bookin; my Beauty School students, collaborators, and new friends; Lucy K Shaw and Poetry Book Club; Dooski McKeon and Poetry Fight Club; and Natalie Eilbert, Chase Berggrun, Ashley Obscura, and Kristen Felicetti, among others. God help us all.

Hell yeah to my father for his quirks, my mother for her stories, and Camille for going first. Hell yeah to the Ryans—Sandy, Dan, Talia, and Glenn—for welcoming me into their family, family group chat, and Duolingo Family Plan. Hell yeah to Esmie, Holmes, Finn, Apa, and Momo for keeping my company company.

Hell yeah to Bug, still; Penny and Nico, there at the foot throughout almost all of this; and Diana and Gio, there now.

Hell yeah to Aidan, best thing, all the way. Oh.

This book is for the hell of it. This book is for all I know. This book is for better and for worse, for reasons that won't escape me, *for all my FAMILY and FRIENDS*, for whomever is concerned. I dedicate it to anyone but not everyone. I dedicate it to you. I dedicate it especially to Lucy Xiang-fu Wainger, little light. Thank you for making so good on your name.

Be good, do good, hell yeah, and go Bills.

Now say it back.

About

Rachelle Toarmino is a poet from Niagara Falls, New York. She is the author of the poetry collections *Hell Yeah* (Third Man Books, 2025) and *That Ex* (Big Lucks Books, 2020), as well as several chapbooks, most recently *My Science* (Sixth Finch Books, 2025), winner of the 2024 Sixth Finch Chapbook Contest. Her work has appeared in *Poets.org*, *Literary Hub*, *Electric Literature*, *American Poetry Review*, *Bennington Review*, *Southeast Review*, *The Slowdown*, and Omnidawn, which awarded her its 2024 Single Poem Broadside Prize. She earned her MFA in poetry at UMass Amherst, where she received an Academy of American Poets Prize. She is also the founding editor in chief of the literary publishing project *Peach Mag* and the creator and lead instructor of Beauty School, an independent poetry school. She lives in Buffalo.